Windows & Stones

An International Poetry Forum Selection

Translated from the Swedish

Windows & Stones

Selected Poems

Tomas Tranströmer

Translated by

May Swenson

with Leif Sjöberg

University of Pittsburgh Press

Most of these poems appeared originally in Sweden under
the following titles:

Mörkerseende (*"Dark Adaptation"*) copyright 1970 by Tomas
Tranströmer; printed by Författarförlaget in Göteborg,
Sweden.

Kvartett (*"Quartet"*) copyright 1966, 1962, 1958, and 1954 by
Tomas Tranströmer; published by Svalans Lyrikklubb,
Albert Bonniers, Stockholm, copyright 1967 by the publisher.
Kvartett is a collected volume of four former books by Tomas
Tranströmer, published by Bonniers and titled as follows:
Klanger och Spår (*"Echoes & Traces"*) 1966; *Den Halvfärdiga
Himlen* (*"The Half-made Heaven"*), 1962; *Hemligheter på
Vägen* (*"Secrets on the Way"*), 1958; *17 Dikter* (*"17 Poems"*),
1954.

Some of these English translations of Tomas Tranströmer's
poems appeared originally in *For W. H. Auden*, a commemora-
tive volume edited by H. Salus and Paul B. Taylor, pub-
lished by Random House, Inc., 1972. Used by permission.

"Five Stanzas to Thoreau" first appeared in *Norden*, Brooklyn,
New York, and is used by permission.

"Secrets on the Way" is reprinted with the permission of
The Times Literary Supplement, London.

Publication of this book has been made possible by

grants to the International Poetry Forum from the

Royal Swedish Embassy, the American-Scandinavian

Foundation, and the A. W. Mellon Educational and

Charitable Trust.

Contents

Foreword

*T*HE hope of the International Poetry Forum is to be no less international than poetry itself. To be sure, such a hope invites certain practical limitations. While poetry has the destiny of speaking to all men at all times, the International Poetry Forum concerns itself with bringing particular poets into contact with as many people as possible right now. While poetry speaks ultimately from and to the common nationality of flesh and blood, the International Poetry Forum attempts in a proximate way to permit poets of different nationalities and alphabets to have their work known and understood by people of nationalities and alphabets other than their own.

To help achieve this goal the International Poetry Forum has initiated a series of foreign selections. These selections not only permit the recognition of deserving poets by a financial award but also provide for the publication of English translations of some of their poems so that many major poets of the world eventually will be known to the English-speaking public.

The Swedish Selection is the third in this series, the first two having been the Turkish Selection to Fazıl Hüsnü Dağlarca in 1968 and the Syria-Lebanon Selection to Adonis (Ali Ahmed Said) in 1971.

SAMUEL HAZO, *Director*
International Poetry Forum

Preface

SIGNALS and responses radiating from our senses (visual, tactile, acoustic, kinetic) give rise to various arts, for instance, painting, sculpture, music, and dance. Poetry, we like to think, combines them all within its matrix of language, while producing an intellectual blossom specifically its own. Fortunate are those arts not dependent on *words*—able to stand free, therefore, in the field of perception anywhere in the world. To be widely "seen," poetry must submit to alteration of its very body with the process of translation—an essentially clumsy and disfiguring act. Why have we not, by now, put together from various linguistic roots so basic a human exchange as one language? For one thing, it could quicken our recognition of one world.

The material body of a poem is its words, and these in a particular language. Not just the meanings of the words, but their tongue-tooled shapes, their rhythms within a certain speech pattern, the echo and shadow behind them of a long sound-and-image history: all this must be conjured—*along with* the import and feeling the words are signals for—to bring the poem whole across the gap between two languages. One soon finds that total transferral is impossible.

What I have tried to do, in these approximations in English of Tomas Tranströmer's Swedish poems, is (1) to feel out and be activated by the central impulse at the root of each poem; (2) to parallel, when possible without awkwardness, the Swedish words, keeping their sequence the same unless English grammar disallowed; (3) to choose, among word alternatives, the closest match for the sense, rhythm, texture, image, and aura of the

Swedish; and (4) to avoid manipulation: not to insert (even unconsciously) something of my own technique into the Englishing of the poems. In general, my aim has been to keep a clear syntactical surface through which Tranströmer's characteristic intentions can be expected to shine.

Some of the riches peculiar to Swedish have had to be forfeited: the frequency of hard consonants which give so strong and exciting a musical texture and the compound words with their immediacy and economy. "Moment" or "instant" in Swedish is *ögonblick*, literally "eye-glance" or "twinkling of an eye." "The void" or "vacancy" is *tomrummet*, "empty room." I particularly regret that such expressions, with their interior metaphors intact, have to be rendered in the abstract in English; otherwise the sense would be obscured. Telescoped words like *flyttfågelsflocken* and *skolpojksmålning* must be taken apart to become "migratory bird flock" and "schoolboy's painting." Too bad that *storflygplats* ("big flying place") must become simply "airfield."

To make up for the loss of certain metrical and other effects, I have taken advantage of lucky accidents offered by English, here and there allowing paired vowel sounds, some alliteration, and occasional casual rhymes when such things happened naturally—being careful, however, not to invent or "improve" anything. A translation may be equivalent as to message, yet may lose its life as a poem unless resources of the new language are put to use.

But there has had to be very little substitution or reorganization. Tranströmer's way with language is direct, without involution, honest. "Truth needs no furniture," he remarks in one of the poems from *Dark Adaptation*. His is a syntax neither in nor out of style; it is free of hyperbole as well as cliché. He has maintained a strong allegiance to his own method and vision—a consistent vision that has become more penetrating with development. In his modes he has moved through quite strict metrics toward more open forms, while never allowing his themes, which are always existential, to become locked into polemics. Tranströmer uses complex states of mind and feeling. The symbolism is individual but not hermetic: one feels a commonality with his meditations and the discoveries arising from them. Almost every poem is a double exposure: objective experience reported in the simplest terms, subjective revelation emerging as simultaneous underimage. For him the poem becomes a kind of divining rod that locates subsurface springs of self-knowledge. The paths taken are fresh—and suspenseful—for they are steep paths through windings of the psyche that most of us let remain vague and dark. He makes a clearing, once dichotomous beauties and ironies have been fought through. When his spring is unearthed, we find it cura- tive of *our* inner half-recognized conflicts too.

The poems in *Windows & Stones* are arranged in reverse chronology. The *stones* in "Guard Duty," the opening poem (written in 1971), significantly recall those other *stones* in his earliest poem here (written in 1948), placed at the end of the selection. *Stone*, the opaque, impenetrable, absolute, and *Window*, opposite symbol of clarity, openness, together with the risk of vulnerabil-

ity—these might be two points of a caliper by which
we can best pick up Tomas Tranströmer's total work.
Other symbols show up recurrently as well. Inanimate
objects are often infused with potent life and archetypal
meaning by this poet.

Tranströmer has read the translations and has
approved the final versions. His comments and, some-
times when my interpretations have been inaccurate, his
specific suggestions have been valuable. As an instance,
in the poem "Twenty-Four Hours" (p. 79) the first line in
Swedish reads:

Stilla vaktar skogsmyran, ser i intet / in.

My first version read:

Unmoving, the ant in the forest keeps watch, / seeing nothing.

Came the letter from Sweden, which said: "*Ser i intet
in* is a little more than *seeing nothing*. The ant is
looking into nothing as if 'nothing' was something,
something you really can look into." It is on such a point,
the inscrutable, that the real poet trains his eye, and to
our benefit.

Some of the poet's letters show sketches in the
margins—of a glass house on the hillside, or horsetail
mushrooms, of a droll Bronze Age trumpet—charming
"visual aids" that bypass the necessity of interlingual
communication. I wish they could have been included
beside the poems.

This selection represents a major portion of Tomas
Tranströmer's published work over more than twenty
years. The new poems that begin the book have not

been collected previously either in Swedish or in translation, and there are sixteen poems here published in English for the first time.

I wish to acknowledge Tomas Tranströmer's cooperation in this translation, together with the expert assistance of Leif Sjöberg, distinguished linguist, who furnished word-for-word transliteration. Otherwise my unschooled knowledge of Swedish would not have been equal to this project. I wish, as well, to thank Samuel Hazo, Director of the International Poetry Forum, which commissioned the work.

MAY SWENSON

Introduction

T OMAS Tranströmer, who was born in Stockholm, Sweden, in 1931, created something of a sensation with his first slim volume *17 Dikter* (*17 Poems*, 1954). Its perfect employment of classical metrics, its startling new discoveries in Swedish landscapes and seascapes, and its amazing density of acute images soon made Tranströmer the most imitated poet in Sweden. As one critic remarked not long ago, it seemed that for some years "everybody heard and saw the same as Tomas Tranströmer."

The point of departure for his nature impressions was usually Runmarö, a small island in the Stockholm skerries, where the poet spent his summers since childhood. In "Storm," one of his mature poems in classical Sapphic meter, Tomas Tranströmer characteristically begins with motion or a sudden transition:

> Suddenly, out walking, he meets the giant
> oak, like an ancient petrified elk, with
> mile-wide crown in front of September's sea,
> the dusk-green fortress.
>
> Storm from the north. When rowanberry
> clusters ripen. Awake in the dark, he hears
> constellations stamping in their stalls, high
> over the oak tree.

In his longest and most ambitious blank verse poem, "Epilogue," there are clear religious overtones. This poem is Tranströmer's attempt to make a long poem similar to T. S. Eliot's *Four Quartets*, but he stops short of completing it as such:

                                 Gust
after gust sweeps over the bay, and out
to the open sea that casts itself into darkness.
   Overhead the stars flash desperately,
   switched on and off by racing clouds

The entire poem is permeated with feverish natural
activity which he heightens with his strong verbs:
"sweeps," "casts itself," "flash," "switched on and off,"
"racing." The mood is excited, yet it is also calm,
objective. In "Epilogue," "God's soul is like the Nile:
it overflows/and dries up." Thus it may either kill off
or create new life, in rhythmic sequence. Tomas
Tranströmer's ambivalence before God is evident in the
line "He is also unchangeable." Thus God is static, an
outworn concept that is no longer relevant to our time.
   While his *17 Dikter* is native in themes, his next
book, *Hemligheter på Vägen* (*Secrets on the Way*, 1958),
is more international. The poems deal with travel and
works of art. They no longer depend totally for their
strength on the landscape of Sweden.
   Den Halvfärdiga Himlen (*The Half-made Heaven*
or *The Half-ready Sky*, 1962), his third book, continues
with further travel impressions of Italy, Greece, and
Egypt. It also contains a few love poems. Music, al-
ways an important source of inspiration to Tomas
Tranströmer, is prevalent in this collection. In addition
to poems with obvious musical titles such as "Nocturne"
and "Allegro," there are other poems which owe a debt
to music. Also in this volume the poet begins to fear
the things which occasionally lead to his depressions

and unproductivity. This fear is evident in "The Palace":

> Softer than the whisper in a shell
> noises and voices from the town
> we heard circling in the empty room,
> muttering in their search for power.
>
> Also something else. Something dark
> stationed itself at the threshold
> of our five senses but couldn't pass.
> Silent sand ran in the hourglass.

Tranströmer is less concerned with form in his fourth book, *Klanger och Spår* (*Echoes & Traces*, 1966). Instead of nature impromptus there are larger, more cohesive statements. The startling juxtapositions with a mystical isolation of phenomena, reminiscent of dream flight, are less frequent than in the earlier collections. The poet is less anonymous. In one poem, "Loneliness," he describes in an almost documentary way a traffic accident threatening his life. This volume also contains poems on Lisbon, Oklahoma, and Central Africa. Furthermore, there is a notable portrait of the popular Norwegian composer, Edvard Grieg, urging himself to "simplify!"

Tranströmer's fifth and latest collection, *Mörkerseende* (*Dark Adaptation*, 1970), displays an even greater simplification of form, and the autobiographical element in these eleven poems is more pronounced than earlier. The poems are entirely documentary, almost confessional. In a friend's copy of the book, he has even explicitly jotted down the names of places and the circumstances under which the experiences occurred.

Mörkerseende, which Robert Bly has translated as *Night Vision* (Ithaca, N. Y.: Lilabulero Press, 1971), and the Scottish poet Robin Fulton has entitled "Seeing in the Dark" (*Lines Review*, 35), reflects a serious crisis or perhaps a series of crises. Tranströmer speaks of great and shattering changes in his personal life, death and disease among his kin, a feeling of lost identity, and worries about the war between technology and nature. "The Bookcase" opens with the line, "It was brought from the dead woman's apartment." The poet, who has been particularly close to his mother (in the absence of a father since childhood, when the parents were divorced), now has to face her death. In "Preludes" he has emptied his mother's apartment, which he, too, has inhabited for the better part of his life. Hope has vanished. "An anchor has let go— / but despite the mournful air it's still the lightest apartment / in the city." The poet can cherish his memories undisturbed, he is more on his own, and he possesses some new, deeper insight: "Truth needs no furniture. I've gone one round / on life's circle and come back to the starting point: / a bare room." His childhood experiences fade in the strong light and give way to concentration on the present. His vision is widened—but also darkened, as the very title "Dark Adaptation" reminds us—and "the windows have / enlarged. The empty apartment is a big telescope pointed at / the sky." Also discernible in "Preludes" is a similar development in which

Tranströmer stresses that efforts to escape from the truth of the self are futile. In a recent poem, "Guard Duty," the idea of the present is reinforced:

> I am whistled back from the distance,
> I crawl out among stones. Here and now.
>
> Mission: to be where I am
> Also, in my silly and solemn role,
> I am the place
> where creation works on itself.

The philistine's concept of a poet as an impractical, impulsive, irresponsible individual with a generally weak human organization could not easily be applied to Tomas Tranströmer. He is a psychologist by profession and from 1960 to 1966 served as counselor to juvenile delinquents at the modern Roxtuna institution, at times having charge of the whole institution. In 1967 he moved with his wife and two daughters to the city of Västerås, where he took a part-time job in order to devote more time to poetry, translations, and readings. He still devotes much of his energy to problem cases in occupational psychology and aptitude tests for handicapped people. Tranströmer frequently participates in conferences of social psychologists, social workers and others, and he has led study groups for probation officers on how to treat prisoners.

Tranströmer has naturally incorporated his experiences as a psychologist into his poems in an unobtrusive, indirect way. In "Winter's Formulae" he writes:

The hospital pavilions
glow against the darkness
like lighted TV screens.

A hidden tuning fork
in the immense cold
emits its ringing hum.

I stand under starry sky
and feel the world crawl
in and out of my coat
as in an ant hill.

As a poet and psychologist Tranströmer is interested
in the subconscious, especially dream intervals and
awakenings; it is notable that many of his poems deal
with awakening.

Fearful of the proliferation of superimposed
patterns of any kind, be they social or political, he has
never worked as a journalist, who expresses and creates
opinions, but keeps very well informed of "what
happens far away." His many travels reflect his urgent
desire for discovery and uncovering of "what happens
in what *seems* to happen." Tranströmer has no doubts
about the task of the poet in our time. He remains
independent of groups or coteries, so that he can
illuminate reality and perceive it as if for the first time.

How did the forceful turn to the left among his
contemporaries affect Tranströmer? "Politics, world
events, society, the power struggle are all inevitable,"
said Tranströmer in an interview (1968). "All of them
are also to be found in my later books. But in youthful
audiences there are always a few who take me to task

for allegedly being 'turned away from the world.' They want me to write in a political way, use political language. Actually they would allow me to write about anything, flowers and bees, as long as I did it in a 'political' way. But the language of poetry, at least the language of my poetry, gets its meaning when it engages itself in a political reality without being politicalized." He defines a politicalized language as one which serves as a means to exert pressure and through which false alternatives are presented, and maintains that "political consciousness includes ability to see through these language patterns; not to subordinate oneself under them."

What does he then expect from poetry? He wants to see the poetic language act as a new communication between experiences, as a catalyst that liberates man instead of restricting him. Above all, poetry should set man's inspiration free, give him a chance to know himself and to discover in himself dimensions the existence of which he had not been aware of before, dimensions which the commercial society does not consider useful, since they cannot be manipulated readily.

Tranströmer acknowledges many American poets as having an effect on his work. At a recent reading in New York, he acknowledged Walt Whitman as a continuing influence. Other Americans who have influenced him are T. S. Eliot, Robert Lowell, Wallace Stevens, Robert Bly, Louis Simpson, Gary Snyder, and James Wright. Indeed, he writes, "Whenever I open an American magazine, there is almost always something of interest to me." Among other poets who have meant much to Tranströmer are Alberti (cf. particularly *Sobre los ángeles*, 1927–28), also Neruda, Jiménez (cf. the poem "Caprichos"), Montale, Lorca, Ungaretti, Pasternak, Sándor Weöres, and others. Of Swedish poets of the 1940s, Ragnar Thoursie has made the strongest impression on Tranströmer.

Tomas Tranströmer is vitally concerned with the state of the world, even though he avoids being dogmatic in any discussion. His is a confident, low-keyed voice which I trust will sound clearly to American readers.

LEIF SJÖBERG

New Poems   1970–1971

Guard Duty

I am ordered out into a pile of stones,
like a noble corpse from the Iron Age.
The others may stay in the tent and sleep,
fanned out like spokes in a wheel.

In the tent presides the stove: a big snake
that has swallowed a gob of flame and hisses.
But it's quiet out here in the spring night
among cold stones waiting for dawn.

Here in the cold I begin to fly
like a shaman: I fly to her body,
the parts left white by the bathing suit—
we were in full sunlight, the moss was warm.

I brush near those warm moments,
but cannot stay there for long.
I am whistled back from the distance,
I crawl out among stones. Here and now.

Mission: to be where I am.
Also, in my silly and solemn role,
I am the place
where creation works on itself.

It dawns. The sparse tree trunks
have color now. The frostbitten forest
flowers send a search party
for anyone who's lost in the dark.

But to be where I am. And wait.
I am anxious, stubborn, confused.
Future events, they already exist!
I know it. They are out there:

a murmuring crowd outside the barricade.
They can only pass one by one.
They want to enter. Why? They come
one by one. I am the turnstile.

To Friends Behind a Border

I
I wrote so stingily to you. But what I didn't dare write
swelled and swelled like an old-fashioned dirigible
and finally sailed away through the night sky.

II
Now my letter is with the censor. He turns on his lamp.
In the beam my words leap like apes onto a grating,
shake it, go stiff, and bare their teeth.

III
Read between the lines. We shall meet in 200 years
when the microphones in the hotel walls, forgotten and
allowed to sleep at last, are imbedded fossils.

Sketch in October

The tugboat is freckled with rust. What is it doing here, far
    inland?
It's a heavy, quenched lamp in the cold.
But the trees wave wild colors: signals to the other shore.
As if wanting to be rescued.

On the way home, horsetail mushrooms I see sprout from the grassy
    turf.
They are the help-asking fingers of one
who long has sobbed by himself in the dark down there.
We are the earth's.

From *Dark Adaptation*   1966–1970

The Name

I get sleepy while driving and turn in under the trees
by the side of the road. Curled up in the back seat
I go to sleep. How long? Long enough for darkness to
fall.

Suddenly I am awake and can't remember who I am. Wide
awake, but it doesn't help. Where am I? WHO am I?
I am something that wakes up in the back seat of a car,
in panic, struggling like a cat in a sack. Who?

Eventually my life comes back to me. My name reappears
like an angel. Outside the walls a trumpet is blown
(as in the *Leonora Overture*) and blessed footsteps come
quick quick down a very long stairway. It is me! It is
me!

What is impossible to forget is those fifteen seconds in
the dark hell of amnesia, a few yards off the main
highway where the traffic with its headlight glare streaks
by.

A Few Minutes

The scrub pine in the marsh presents its crown: a dark rag.
But what you see is nothing
compared to the roots, the outspreading, secretly creeping,
    immortal
                          or half-immortal root system.

I you she he branching out also . . .
Beyond what was intended.
Beyond our Metropolis.

From the milk-white summer sky darts a rain.
It feels like my five senses are yoked to another being
who stubbornly moves on,
like the white-clad lap-racers in a stadium, darkness sifting down.

Breathing Room: July

Lying on his back under tall trees
he is also up there. He rills into thousands of twigs and branches,
is swayed back and forth,
as if in a catapult seat outflung in slow motion.

Standing down by the jetties he squints across the waters.
The docks age sooner than men.
Made of splintered silver gray planks, and with stones in their
        bellies.
The blinding light rips its way straight through.

Sailing all day in an open boat
over the glittering bights,
he will fall asleep at last inside a blue lamp
while islands like great nocturnal moths creep over the glass.

Traffic

The long-distance truck with its trailer pushes through fog,
the huge silhouette of a dragonfly's larva
slowly stirring the silt on the lake's bottom.

Our headlamps meet in the dripping gloom.
We can't make out each other's faces.
Floods of light plunge through pine needles.

We come, we shadowy vans from all directions,
in twilight, in tandem, shuttling single file,
gliding forward in a muffled, turned-down roar

out on the flats where industries brood,
and the building developments sink two millimeters
a year—the ground slowly swallows them.

Unidentified paws put their prints
on the shiniest product dreamed up around here.
Seeds struggle to live in the asphalt.

But first the chestnut trees go murky, as if
preparing a blossoming of iron gloves
instead of white catkins, while behind them

in the company's front office a faulty neon tube
keeps blinking blinking. There's a secret door here. Open!
and put your eye to the reversed periscope,

look down, into the gullets, into the lowest drains
where algae thrive like dead men's beards,
where The Cleaner swims in his coverall of slime

with ever feebler strokes, about to suffocate.
And no one knows how it will turn out, only that the chain
breaks and is mended again, over and over.

Night Work

I

Tonight I'm below with the ballast.
I am one of those dumbweights
keeping the ship from tipping over!
Indistinct faces in the dark like stones.
They can only hiss: "Don't touch me."

II

Other voices crowd close, as the listener
slips like a thin shadow over the radio's
luminous broadcasting band.
Language is step in step with the executioners.
Therefore we must adopt a new language.

III

The wolf is here, our all-time friend,
he's testing the windows with his tongue.
The valley is crawling with ax handles.
Noise of night planes spills from the sky
sluggishly, as from a wheelchair with iron casters.

IV

The city is being dug up. But it's quiet just now.
Under the elms in the churchyard,
an idle bulldozer—its jaw on the ground,
like someone fallen asleep at the table,
fist in front of his forehead. —Clocks chiming.

The Open Window

I was shaving one morning
by the open window
one flight up.
Switched the razor on.
It began to buzz.
Buzzed louder and louder.
Increased to a roar.
Enlarged to a helicopter,
and a voice—the pilot's—penetrated
the roar, shrieking:
"All eyes open!
You see this for the last time."
We lifted off.
Flew low over summertime.
So many things I loved, have they no significance?
Dozens of dialects of green.
And especially the red of the timbered house-walls.
Beetles that gleamed in dung, in sun.
Cellars pulled up by the roots
came through the air.

Things happening.
Printing presses crawling.
Just now people were
the only ones keeping still.
They observed a minute of silence.
Especially the dead in the churchyard
held still
as when posing for a picture in the camera's childhood.

Fly low!
I didn't know which way
to turn my head—
to see both sides
like a horse.

Preludes

I
I flinch from something that shuffles slantwise through sleet.
A fragment of what is to come.
A wall broken loose. Something without eyes. Hard.
A face of teeth!
A lone wall. Or is the house there
although I do not see it?
The Future: an army of empty houses
that grope their way ahead through sleet.

II
Two truths approach each other. One comes from within,
one comes from without—and where they meet you have the chance
to catch a look at yourself.
Noticing what is about to happen, you shout desperately: "Stop!
Anything, anything, as long as I don't have to know myself."

And there is a boat that wants to put in—tries to, right here—
it will try again thousands of times.
Out of the forest's dark comes a long boat hook
that's pushed through the open window
among the party guests who have danced themselves warm.

III

The apartment I've lived in most of my life is to be evacuated.
It's already emptied of everything. An anchor has let go—
but despite the mournful air it's still the lightest apartment
in the city. Truth needs no furniture. I've gone one round
on life's circle and come back to the starting point:
a bare room. Scenes from my early life take shape on the walls
like Egyptian paintings inside a burial chamber. But they
are fading. The light is too strong. The windows have
enlarged. The empty apartment is a big telescope pointed at
the sky. It's as quiet here as a Quaker meeting. Nothing heard
but the pigeons of the backyards, their cooings.

Upright

In a moment of concentration I was able to catch the hen,
and stood with it in my hands. Strange, it didn't feel
really alive: stiff, dry, a white feather-plumed old lady's
hat squawking truths from 1912. Thunder hovered in the air.
From the floorboards wafted an odor like that trapped
between covers of a photo album so ancient that the portraits
can no longer be identified.

I carried the hen to her yard and let her go. She came
suddenly to life, recognized herself, and began racing around
according to the old order. The henyard is full of taboos.
But outside, the ground is loaded with love and *sisu*.*
Half overgrown with bushes and vines, a low stone wall.
At dusk the stones begin to emanate light from the century-old
warmth of the hands that piled them.

The winter has been hard, but it is summer now, and the soil
wants us to stay upright. Free but attentive, as when
standing up in a small boat. There leaps to mind a memory
from Africa: the shore at Chari: many boats, a most friendly
atmosphere, the nearly blue black people with three parallel
scars on each cheek (the SARA tribe.) I am welcomed aboard—
a canoe of darkest wood. It is extremely unsteady, even
when I crouch on my heels. The act of balance. If the heart
is on the left, lean the head slightly to the right, keep
your pockets empty, make no big gestures—leave all
rhetoric behind. That's it: rhetoric is impossible here.
The canoe skims over the water.

* Finnish, meaning "energy," or "stamina."

18

The Bookcase

It was brought from the dead woman's apartment. It stood
empty a few days, empty until I filled it with books, all the
bound ones, those bulky tomes. With that act I had let in
the underworld. Something swelled up from below, mounted
slowly, inexorably, like mercury in a gigantic thermometer.
You must not turn your head away.

The swarthy volumes, their closed faces. They're like the
Algerians who stood at the Friedrichstrasse border crossing,
waiting for the *Volkspolizei* to check their passports. My own
passport lay a long time in various glass cubicles. And
the fog all over Berlin that day, it is also in this book-
case. An old despair lives in there, it tastes of
Passchendaele* and the Treaty of Versailles—the taste, in
fact, is older than that. The black heavy tomes—I come
back to them—they are themselves a sort of passport, and
they are so fat because they have accumulated so many stamps
through the centuries. There is one trip, apparently, for
which your baggage can't be heavy enough, once you've
embarked, when finally you . . .

All the old historians are there, and are invited to
climb up and look into our family. Nothing can be heard,
but the lips move all the time behind the glass ("Passchen-
daele" . . .). One is reminded of a venerable government office

---

* Place in Belgium, scene of battle, World War I.

—now follows a true ghost story—a grand building where portraits of long-dead men hang behind glass, and one morning there appeared a blur on the inside of the glass. They had begun breathing during the night.

The bookcase is even more powerful. Glares straight across the zone boundary! A shimmering membrane, the shimmering membrane of a dark river in which the room is forced to mirror itself. And you must not turn your head away.

From *Echoes & Traces*   1963–1966

Winter's Formulae

I

I went to sleep in my bed
and awoke under the keel.

In the morning, four o'clock,
when bones, scoured clean,
collect together coldly.

I went to sleep among swallows
and awoke among eagles.

II

In lamplight, ice on the road
glistens like lard.

This is not Africa.
This is not Europe.
This is nowhere but "here."

And what was "I"
is only a word
in December's dark mouth.

III

The hospital pavilions
glow against the darkness
like lighted TV screens.

A hidden tuning fork
in the immense cold
emits its ringing hum.

I stand under starry sky
and feel the world crawl
in and out of my coat
as in an anthill.

IV

Three black oaks jut from snow.
So rough, but nimble-fingered.
From their ample bottles
verdure will foam this spring.

V

The bus crawls through winter dusk
like a ship aglow among pines
where the road is a narrow, deep, dead canal.

Few passengers: some old, some youngsters.
If the bus should stop, lights out,
the whole world would black out.

Oklahoma

I

The train stalled far to the south. Snow in New York,
but here we could go in shirtsleeves all night.
Yet no one was out. Only the cars
sped by in flashes of light like flying saucers.

II

"We battlegrounds are proud
of our many dead . . ."
said a voice as I awakened.

The man behind the counter said:
"I'm not trying to sell anything,
I'm not trying to sell anything,
I just want you to see something."
And he displayed the Indian axes.

The boy said:
"I know I have a prejudice,
I don't want to have it, sir.
What do you think of us?"

III

This motel is a foreign shell. With a rented car
(like a big white servant) outside the door.
Nearly devoid of memory, and without profession,
I let myself sink to my midpoint.

Summer Plain

We have seen so much.
Reality has almost used us up,
but here is summer at last:

a jet airport. The flight controller
brings load after load of frozen
human beings down from space.

The grass and the flowers—here we land.
The grass has a green chief.
I report myself to him.

Under Pressure

Blue heaven's engine drone is strong.
We are on a construction site amid vibration,
where the ocean floor may suddenly upheave—
conches and telephones whispering.

Beauty is something snatched briefly from the side.
The dense crop in the field, various shades of
the gold swathe.
Turbulent shadows in my head are attracted to it.
They would like to melt into the crop and
become yellow.

Darkness falls. At midnight I go to bed.
The smaller boat is set apart from the bigger boat.
Alone on the water.
Society's dark hull glides farther and farther out.

Open and Closed Rooms

A man touches the world with his trade for a glove.
He rests in the middle of the day leaving his gloves
                              on the shelf.
They suddenly start to grow, inflate themselves
and darken the whole house from the inside.

The darkened house sits surrounded by soft spring winds.
"Amnesty," is the whisper of the grass: "Amnesty."
A boy runs with an invisible string that slants
                         right up into heaven
where his wild dream of the future soars, a kite
                         bigger than the suburb.

Farther north, seen from the hilltop, is an endless blue
                              sprucewood carpet
where the shadows of clouds
stand still.
No, *fly on.*

An Artist in the North

I, Edvard Grieg, moved free among men.
I joked a lot, read the papers, often on tour.
I conducted the orchestra.
The auditorium and its lights shuddered with each triumph
                    like a train ferry pushing in to dock.

I have holed myself up here to butt heads with silence.
My work hut is small.
The grand piano fits as rubbing-tight in here as a swallow
                    under a roof shingle.

The steep and lovely mountain slopes are silent most of the time.
There is no path
but there is a wicket that sometimes opens,
and a peculiar light leaks in directly from the trolls.

Simplify!

And hammer blows in the mountain came
came
came
came one spring night into our room
disguised as heartbeats.

The year before I die I shall send out four hymns
                    to track down God.
But it begins here.
A song about that which is near.

That which is near.

Battlegrounds within us
where we Bones of the Dead
fight to come alive.

In the Clear

I

Late autumn labyrinth.
On the threshold of the forest a discarded empty bottle.
Go in. The forest is still, its rooms vacant now.
Just a few small sounds: like someone carefully moving twigs
              here and there with a clipper,
or like a hinge squeaking faintly inside a thick trunk.
Frost has breathed on the mushrooms and they have shriveled.
They look like objects or clothes left behind by
              missing persons.
Now comes the twilight. It's a matter of finding the way out
and locating some landmarks: that rusty implement
              in the field,
and the house across the lake, a red brown square,
              concentrated as a bouillon cube.

II

A letter from America got me going, drove me out
into the white night of June on lonely suburban streets
among new buildings, naked of memory, cool as blueprints.
Letter in pocket. Restless, furious walking—it is a
              kind of expiation.
Where you are, evil and good have opposite faces.
With us it is mainly a confusion of roots, numbers, lights.

They who do death's errands are not afraid of daylight.
They govern from glass apartments. They swarm in sun blaze.
They lean forward over the counter and turn their heads.

Farther on, I happen to stop by one of the new facades.
Many windows flow together into one window.
The night sky's light is trapped there and the treetops'
                              tossing.
It is a vertical lake without waves, reflecting
                         the summer night.

Violence for a moment
feels unreal.

III

The sun blazes. The jet plane glides at low altitude
and casts a shadow in the shape of a big cross
                              that rushes over the ground.
A man hunches in a field and digs.
The shadow comes.
For a fraction of a second he is in the middle of the cross.

I have seen the cross hanging in cool church vaultings—
sometimes it's like an instantaneous photograph
of something in rapid motion.

From *The Half-made Heaven*   1958–1962

The Couple

They snuff the lamp, and its white mantle shimmers
a moment before the last light dissolves
like a tablet in the glass of night. Then they soar.
The hotel walls shoot up to the dark sky.

Passion's motions dwindle, and they sleep,
but their most secret thoughts connect,
as when two colors meet and interflow
on the wet paper of a schoolboy's painting.

All is dark and still. But the town pushes closer
tonight. With quenched windows. Houses have come.
They stand in a huddle, massed together,
a waiting crowd with unexpressive faces.

Tree and Sky

A tree is walking in the rain,
hurrying past us in the splattering gray.
It has an errand. It takes life from the rain
like a blackbird in an orchard.

When the rain is over, the tree stops.
Dim, unstirring, erect on clear nights
it waits as we do for the moment
when snowflakes will burst from space.

Face to Face

In February life stood still.
Birds unwilling to fly, and I
chafed at the landscape like a boat
that rubs the jetty it's tied to.

Trees stood with backs turned all one way.
Snow depth was measured by dead straws.
Footprints aged out there on the crust.
Under the pall even language faded.

One day something came up to the window.
Work stopped. I looked up.
Colors burned. Everything turned around.
The ground and I sprang at each other.

In the Forest

A place that we call Jacob's Marsh
is the summer day's cellar
where light sours like a drink
tasting of age and slums.

Weak giants stand there snarled
so dense that none can fall.
The cracked birch molders there
in a posture upright as dogma.

From the bottom land I climb.
It brightens between the trunks.
It rains over all my roofs.
I am a spout for sensations.

At the wood's edge, air fresh and mild.—
Great fir, arrogant, dark,
your muzzle deep in humus,
you drink shadow from the rain.

Journey

On the subway platform.
A crowd among billboards
in a staring dead light.

The train comes and fetches
faces and briefcases.

Darkness next. We sit
like statues in the cars
hauled into the tunnels.
Strain, dreams, strain.

At stations below sea level
is sold the news of darkness.
People moving melancholy,
mum, beneath clockfaces.

The train carries a load
of street clothes and souls.

Looks in all directions,
passing through the mountain.
Nothing changing yet.

But near the surface begins
the hum of freedom's bees.
We emerge from the earth.

The countryside flaps wings
once, and then subsides
under us, wide and greenish.

Shucks of corn blow in
across the platforms.

End of the line! I ride
beyond the end of the line.

How many aboard? Four,
five, hardly more.

Houses, roads, skies,
fjords, mountains
open their windows.

Espresso

Black coffee at sidewalk cafés
with chairs and tables like gaudy insects.

It is a precious sip we intercept
filled with the same strength as Yes and No.

It is fetched out of gloomy kitchens
and looks into the sun without blinking.

In daylight a dot of wholesome black
quickly drained by the wan patron . . .

Like those black drops of profundity
sometimes absorbed by the soul

that give us a healthy push: Go!
The courage to open our eyes.

From the Mountain

I stand on the mountain looking at water.
Boats loiter on the surface of summer.
"We are somnambulists. Moons adrift."
So say the white sails.

"We sneak through a sleeping house.
We slowly shove open the doors.
We lean against freedom."
So say the white sails.

Once I saw the world's hopes sailing.
They plied the same course—as one fleet.
"We are scattered now. No one's retinue."
So say the white sails.

The Palace

We went in. An enormous hall,
hushed, vacant, the floor bare,
all one plank smooth as ice.
The doors closed. The air, gray.

Paintings on the walls. We saw
swarming still lifes: shields, scale-
pans, fish, wriggling struggling forms
competing in a deaf-mute mirror world.

A sculpture was installed in space:
alone and central stood a horse,
but we didn't notice him at first,
we were wonder struck by vacancy.

Softer than the whisper in a shell
noises and voices from the town
we heard circling in the empty room,
muttering in their search for power.

Also something else. Something dark
stationed itself at the threshold
of our five senses but couldn't pass.
Silent sand ran in the hourglass.

Time we bestirred ourselves. We moved
toward the horse. He was gigantic,
black as iron. The image of power itself,
still here, though sovereigns have vanished.

The horse spoke: "I am the Only One.
The vacancy that rode me I have thrown.
This is my stable. I am growing slowly.
And I eat the silence here."

Syros

In Syros' harbor abandoned merchant ships lay idle.
Stem by stem by stem. Moored for many years:
CAPE RION, Monrovia.
KRITOS, Andros.
SCOTIA, Panama.

Dark paintings on the water, they have been hung aside.

Like playthings from our childhood, grown gigantic,
that remind us
of what we never became.

XELATROS, Piraeus.
CASSIOPEIA, Monrovia.
The ocean scans them no more.

But when we first came to Syros, it was at night,
we saw stem by stem by stem in moonlight and thought:
what a powerful fleet, what splendid connections!

A Swimming Dark Figure

About a prehistoric pictograph
on a cliff in the Sahara:
a swimming dark figure
in an ancient river young.

Without weapon or strategy,
neither at rest nor leaping,
and split from his own shadow:
he glides the bed of the stream.

He has struggled to be free
of the slumbering green scene,
to gain the shore at last
and merge with his shadow.

Lamento

He put down his pen.
It lies inert on the table.
It lies inert in space.
He put down his pen.

Too much that can neither be revealed nor concealed!
He's blocked by what's happening elsewhere, apart,
although the magic satchel is throbbing like a heart.

Outdoors it is early summer.
From the greenwood come whistles—of humans or
birds?
And cherry boughs in blossom tap the tops of
trucks that have come home.

Weeks go by.
Night slowly comes.
Moths settle on the windowpane:
small pale telegrams from the world.

Allegro

I play Haydn after a black day
and feel a simple warmth in my hands.

The keyboard is willing. Mild hammers strike.
The sound is green, lively, tranquil.

The sound says that freedom exists,
that someone does not pay Caesar's tax.

I put my hands in my Haydn-pockets
and pretend to take a cool look at the world.

I hoist the Haydn-flag—it indicates:
"We won't surrender. But want peace."

Music is a glass house on the hillside
where stones fly, stones crash.

And the stones crash straight through glass,
but the house remains whole.

The Half-made Heaven

Despair breaks its course.
Anxiety breaks its course.
The vulture breaks his flight.

Dazzling light pours forth—
even the ghosts take a gulp.

Our images, red-painted beasts
in the glacial cave, see day.

Everything stares nakedly around.
We walk in the sun by the hundreds.

Each one is a half-open door
that leads to a room for all.

Unfathomable ground under us.

Water glitters between the trees.

The lake is a window into the earth.

Nocturne

I drive through a village at night, houses step forward
into the headlamps' stream—they are awake, and are thirsty.
Houses, barns, billboards, driverless vehicles—it is now
they clothe themselves with Life. —The population sleeps:

some in peaceful sleep, others with strained features
as if they were entered in hard training for eternity.
They dare not let go of everything even in deepest sleep.
They rest like lowered barriers while the mystery rides by.

Beyond the village the road runs along between forest trees.
And trees trees tramp in silent concord side by side.
They have a theatrical look, as if seen by firelight.
Every leaf distinct! They follow me all the way home.

I lie down ready for sleep, I see the queerest pictures
and signs that scrawl themselves behind my eyelids
on the dark's wall. In a slot between waking and dream
a very large envelope tries in vain to push itself through.

From *Secrets on the Way*   1954–1958

Awakening to Song Over the Rooftops

Morning, May rain. City in double stillness
like a mountain village. Streets silent.
Aloft, the blue green buzz of an aircraft engine.—
      The window is open.

Dream in which the sleeper lies outstretched
becomes transparent. He bestirs himself, begins
to fumble for his tool kit of attention.—
      Almost within reach.

Weather Picture

October's sea flashes its cold
dorsal fin of mirages.

Nothing's left that remembers
the racing sails' white dizziness.

An amber ray over the village.
And all sounds in slow flight.

Dog's bark, a hieroglyph, appears
in air above the garden

where the yellow pear outwits
the tree, lets itself fall.

The Four Temperaments

The scanning eye turns sunbeams into billy clubs.
And in the evening: hubbub of a party upstairs
erupts like artificial flowers through the floor.

Crossed the plain. Darkness. Wagon apparently stuck.
An antibird shrieked in the star void.
Albino sun stood over the chopped dark sea.

*

A man like an uprooted tree with croaking leaves
and a lightning bolt at salute saw the whiff-of-wild-beast
sun shoot up through ruffling wings on the world's

rock island speeding behind flags of foam through night
and day the white seafowl yelling
on deck and all with tickets to Chaos.

*

You've merely to shut your eyes to hear clearly
the sea gulls tolling Sunday through ocean's endless parish.
A guitar starts plucking in the thicket, a cloud shifts

idly as late-come spring's green sleigh
—the whinny of light between the shafts—
glides forward on the ice.

*

Woke up with the girlfriend's heels clicking in the dream
and, outside, a pair of snowdrifts like winter's lost gloves,
while handbills from the sun drifted down over the city.

Road never ends. Horizon races outward.
Birds shake in the tree. Dust whirls in the wheels.
All the rolling wheels that contradict death!

Caprichos*

Twilight in Huelva: sooty palm trees
and fleet train whistles
like silver-haired bats.

The streets have been clogged with people.
A lady skimming through the crowd weighs carefully
the last ray of day on her eye's scale.

Office windows open. Still heard
is the tread of the horse inside.
The old horse with rubber stamps for hoofs.

Not until after midnight do the streets empty.
At last all the offices fill up with blue.

Up there in space:
trotting in silence, glistening and black,
unseen, unharnessed,
the rider thrown off:
a new constellation which I name "The Horse."

* Spanish, meaning "whims" or "fancies." Also, the title of one
of Goya's series of etchings.

Siesta

Whitsuntide of the stones. And with crackling tongues ...
The city suspended in the spaciousness of noon.
Interment in simmering light. The drum that drowns out
eternity's locked and pounding fists.

The eagle soars up and up over the sleepers.
A sleep where the mill wheel rumbles like thunder.
Thump of the horse with the blindfolded eyes.
Eternity's locked and pounding fists.

The sleepers are weights hung in the tyrant's clock.
The eagle drifts dead in the sun's white cataract.
And echoing through time—as in Lazarus' burial box—
eternity's locked and pounding fists.

Secrets on the Way

Day's light hit the face of the sleeper.
He had a livelier dream
but did not wake.

Night's dark hit the face of the stroller
out among others under the sun's
strong impatient rays.

Sudden darkness as before a hurricane.
I stood in a room where all moments are kept—
a butterfly museum.

And the sun was as strong as before.
Its impatient brushes painted the world.

Tracks

Night, two o'clock: moonlight. The train has stopped
in the middle of the plain. Distant bright points of a town
twinkle cold on the horizon.

As when someone has gone into a dream so far
that he'll never remember he was there
when he comes back to his room.

And as when someone goes into a sickness so deep
that all his former days become twinkling points, a swarm,
cold and feeble on the horizon.

The train stands perfectly still.
Two o'clock: full moonlight, few stars.

A Man from Benin

On a photograph of a sixteenth-century
bronze relief (from the West African
kingdom of Benin) representing a
Portuguese Jew.

Darkness fell. I was still,
but my shadow thumped
the drum of despair.
When the beating ceased
I saw the image of an image
of a man who arose
from the void
of an opened book.
As one goes past a house
long empty, and sees
someone in the window.
A stranger. A pilot.
Alert and vigilant.
Came near without a step.
Wore a cupped hat
shaped like our hemisphere,
the brim at the equator.
Hair divided in two fins.
A curly beard hung like
eloquence round his mouth.
Held his right arm bent.
It was slender as a child's.
The falcon that should sit there
was realized instead
in his features.

An ambassador.
Cut off in a speech
which silence prolongs
with a greater power.
Three tribes were silent in him.
He was three people's image.
A Jew from Portugal
embarked with the others,
the drifting and waiting
flock that huddled
in the wooden caravel
that was their rocking mother.
Landed in a foreign scent
that made the air shaggy.
Was seen in the marketplace
by a Negro metal-caster,
and long detained in his eyes.
Reborn in the bronze race:
*"I have come to meet
whoever lifts his light
to see himself in me."*

Balakirev's Dream

(1905)

The black grand piano, the shiny spider,
trembled in the center of its net of music.

In the concert hall was conjured a land
where the stones were no heavier than dew.

But Balakirev* fell asleep during the music
and dreamed a dream about the Tzar's droshky.†

It wheeled out over the cobblestones
straight into the crow-cawing dark.

Alone he sat in the carriage, looking out,
at the same time he ran beside it on the road.

He knew the journey had gone on for long,
and his watch showed years, not hours.

There was a field where the plough lay
and the plough was a bird that had fallen.

There was an inlet where the vessel lay
icebound, lights out, the crew on deck.

The droshky raced out on the ice, the wheels
spun and spun with the sound of silk.

A minor man-of-war: "Sevastopol."
He stood on board. The crew came forward.

* Milij Balakirev: Russian composer (1837–1910).
† Horsedrawn four-wheeled carriage used in Russia.

63

"Your life is spared if you can play."
They showed him a fabulous instrument.

It was like a tuba or a phonograph
or part of some unknown engine.

Helpless with fear, he understood: this
was the piston that drove the man-of-war.

He turned and faced the nearest sailor,
made desperate signs with his hands, and begged:

"Make the sign of the cross, make the cross!"
The sailor's eyes turned sad as a blind man's,

his arms stretched out, his head dropped forward—
there he hung as if nailed in the air.

The drums beat. The drums beat. Applause!
Balakirev woke up from his dream.

Wings of applause flapped in the hall.
He saw the man at the grand get up.

In the street was blackout because of the strike.
Droshkies wheeled by swiftly in the night.

After an Attack

The sick boy.
Vise-gripped in a vision
with tongue stiff as a horn.

He sits with his back turned to the picture of the cornfield.
The bandage around the jaw makes you think of embalming.
His glasses are thick as a frogman's. Everything is numb,
yet tense, as when the phone rings at night.

But the picture behind. A soothing landscape, yet the crop
                    is a golden storm.
Blueweed-blue sky and drifting clouds. Beneath, in the yellow surf,
sail some white shirts: reapers—they cast no shadows.

Far off in the field stands a man who seems to look this way.
A broad hat obscures his face.
He seems intent on the dark figure here in the room,
                    as if offering help.
Imperceptibly the picture begins to widen and open behind the
      sick,
preoccupied boy. It glints and vibrates. Each ear is lit
                    as if to arouse him!
The other one—in the cornfield—makes a sign.

He comes closer.
No one sees this.

From *17 Poems*   1948–1953

Prelude

Awakening is a parachute jump from the dream.
Freed from the choking vortex, the diver
sinks toward the green map of morning.
Things magnify. He sees, from the fluttering lark's
position, huge tree-root systems
like branchings of subterranean chandeliers. Above ground,
in tropical flood, earth's greenery
stands with lifted arms, as if listening
to the beat of invisible pistons. And he
sinks toward summer, is lowered
into its dazzling crater, lowered
between fissures of moist green eons
trembling under the sun's turbine. Then halts
the downward dive through time's eyeblink, the wingspread
becomes an osprey's glide over streaming water.
Bronze Age trumpets:
their outlaw tune
hangs motionless over the void.

In the day's first hours consciousness can own the world
like a hand enclosing a sun-warm stone.
The skydiver stands under the tree.
With the plunge through death's vortex
will light's great chute spread over his head?

Autumn in the Skerries

Storm

Suddenly, out walking, he meets the giant
oak, like an ancient petrified elk, with
mile-wide crown in front of September's sea,
> the dusk-green fortress.

Storm from the north. When rowanberry
clusters ripen. Awake in the dark, he hears
constellations stamping in their stalls, high
> over the oak tree.

Evening–Morning

The moon's mast has rotted and the sail shriveled.
A gull soars drunkenly over the sea.
The jetty's thick quadrangle is charred. Brush
> bends low in the dusk.

Out on the doorstep. Daybreak slams and slams in
the sea's gray stone gateway, and the sun flashes
close to the world. Half-choked summer gods
> fumble in sea mist.

Ostinato

Under the buzzard's circling dot of stillness
race the waves roaring into the light,
chewing on their bridles of seaweed, snorting
> froth across the shore.

Land is blind in darkness where the bats
take bearings. The buzzard stops and becomes a star.
Sea races roaring forth and snorts
> froth across the shore.

Five Stanzas to Thoreau

One more has fled the heavy city,
its ring of starved stones. Clear and salty are
the waters that immerse all
    rebels' heads.

In a lazy spiral silence ascends
from earth's navel, takes root here, and grows
a thick crown of leaves to dapple
    the sun-warm stairway.

    *

Absently the foot kicks a mushroom. A thundercloud
swells on the horizon. Like trumpets
the trees' twisted roots vibrate, the leaves
    flutter apart startled.

Autumn's wild passing is a flimsy cape,
the folds blowing until, out of frost and ash,
a flock of calm days comes again, to bathe
    claws in the spring.

    *

No one believes it, that you have seen a geyser,
fled the stagnant well like Thoreau, and that you know
how to vanish deep into your own greenwood,
    crafty and hopeful.

Gogol

Jacket thin and shabby as a wolf pack.
Face like a chip of marble.
Sits encircled by his letters in a copse that whispers
of scorn and error.
Yes, the heart is swept like paper through indifferent
passageways.

Now sneaks the sunset like a fox across this land,
sets fire to the grass in no time.
The air is full of horns and cloven hooves, and underneath
glides the calash* like a shadow over father's
lit-up farmyards.

Petersburg situated at the same latitude as annihilation,
(did you see the fair lady in the leaning tower)
among ice-slabbed houses hovers, like a jellyfish,
the wretch in his overcoat.

Wrapped in his fasts is he who used to run with laughter's herds—
they have long since moved to a range above the tree line.

Man's staggering tables.
Look up, see how darkness brands a Milky Way of souls.
So climb into your fire carriage and leave the country!

* Light two-wheeled horsedrawn vehicle with folding top.

Sailor's Yarn

There are bare winter days when the sea resembles
ranges of mountains, humped in gray feathers,
a moment blue, then long hours of waves. Pallid as
lynx, they seek and fail their grip in the shore's gravel.

On such days wrecked ships leave the sea to find
their masters seated in the city's noise, and crews
long drowned drift ashore, transparent as pipe smoke.

(In the north flits the real lynx, with shining claws
and dream-blue eyes. In the north where time
lives in a mine all day, all night.

There a single survivor may sit
by the northern lights' oven, and listen
to the music of freezers-to-death.)

Strophe and Antistrophe

The outermost circle belongs to myth. There sinks
    the helmsman
erect among glittering spines of fish.
How far away from us! When the day
suffocates in windless unrest—
like the Congo's green shadow holds
the blue men in its vapor—
when all of this flotsam on the heart's slow
twining river
piles itself up.

Sudden change: beneath the float of heavenly hulls
glide the tethered ones.
Stern high, at an impossible angle,
leans the carcass of a dream, black
against a pale red strip of coast. Deserted,
the years drop downhill, quick
and silent as sled shadows, doglike, enormous,
run over snow,
reach the forest.

Agitated Meditation

A storm makes the vanes of the mill whiz around
in night's darkness grinding nothing. —You
       keep awake by the same logic.
The gray shark's belly is your faint lamp.

Vague memories sink to the ocean's floor
and stiffen there—unfamiliar statues. —Green
       with algae is your crutch. He who
wanders to the sea returns petrified.

Connection

See that gray tree. Infinity has trickled
through its fibers into the ground—
a diminished sky is left when
earth has drunk. Stolen space
is woven into the web of roots, braided
to become greenery.   —These brief moments
of freedom escape from us, whirl
through the Norns' blood, and further.

Morning and Entrance

Black-backed gull, the sun-skipper, steers his course.
Under him is wide water.
The world still sleeps like a
many-colored stone in the water.
Undeciphered day. Days—
like Aztec hieroglyphs!

The music. And I stand captive
in its Gobelin tapestry, with
upraised arms—like a figure
from primitive art.

In the Rushing Stem Is Rest

A winter morning shows how the earth
flings itself forward. Against the house walls
rustles a current of air
from the unknown.

Wrapped in motion: calm's tent.
The secret rudder in the migratory bird flock.
Out of winter's dusk
the rising tremolo

from hidden instruments. Like standing under
summer's tall linden tree, tens of thousands of
insect wings
whirring overhead.

Twenty-Four Hours

Unmoving, the ant in the forest looks into
nothing. And nothing is heard but the ticking
of dark greenery, nightlong the murmur deep
                    in summer's chasm.

The spruce tree at point, like a clock's jagged
hand. The ant aglow in the mountain's shadow.
A bird screams! At last. Slowly the cloud cart
                    begins to roll.

Epilogue

December. Sweden is a hauled-up,
unrigged ship. Stark in twilight stand
her masts. And twilight lasts longer
than day. The way here is stony:
not until noon comes daylight,
when winter's colosseum is revealed,
lit by unreal clouds. Then suddenly
the white smoke climbs, twirling up
from the villages. Endlessly high, the clouds.
The sea gropes at heaven's root,
preoccupied and as if listening to something.
(Obscure journeys over the soul's dark,
half-averted the bird that could arouse
the sleeper with its chirp. Then the glass
is shifted, showing another time:
it is summer, the mountains bellow, swollen
with light, the brook carries the sun's glitter
in its transparent hand. . . . But all vanishes,
as when a filmstrip ends in the dark.)

Now burns the evening star through cloud.
Trees, fences and houses grow, grow larger
with the dark's soundless, steepening fall.
And under the star is outlined clear and clearer
the other, secret landscape that lives
the life of contour on night's X-ray plate.
A shadow draws its sled between the houses.
They wait.

Six P.M., and the wind comes
springing with its noise along the street,
bursting into the dark like a pack of horsemen.
How the black disruption jangles, then dies down.
Dancing in place the houses stand, stricken
in this roar that is like a dream's. Gust
after gust sweeps over the bay, and out
to the open sea that casts itself into darkness.
Overhead the stars flash desperately,
switched on and off by racing clouds
which, only when they veil the light, reveal
their presence, like those clouds of the past
that wander through the soul. When I
pass the stable road I hear through the din
the sick horse's stamping from within.

The turning point in the storm is marked
by a broken gate that slams and slams, a lantern
that dangles from a hand, some beast that wails
afraid on the mountain. Retreating, thunder
tumbles over the cow-house roofs, twanging
telephone wires, forcing piercing whistles
from every tile and panel of the night,
and the helpless trees throw their branches.

There escapes a tune from the bagpipes!
A bagpipe tune approaches, with its skirl
of freedom. A procession. A wood on the march!
A splashing around a prow, and darkness shifts,

land and water travel. And the dead
who have gone below deck, they are here,
with us on our way: a voyage, a crossing
that is not tempestuous but calm.

And the world constantly pitches its tent
anew. A summer day, and the wind takes hold
of the oak's tackle and hauls up the earth.
The water lily paddles on its hidden web foot
within the tarn's swift dark embrace.
A boulder is rolled away from the rim of space.

In summer twilight the islands rise
above the horizon. The old villages withdraw,
are on their way deeper into the woods,
with the season's wheel, the magpie's squawk.
When the year kicks off its boots
and the sun shinnies higher, trees take leaf,
are filled with wind and sail out freely.
At the mountain's foot the burnt and blasted pinewood,
but summer's long tepid surf will come,
drag through the fallen treetops slowly, rest
a moment, then sink lower, and recede,
leaving the leafless beach. And ultimately
God's soul is like the Nile: it overflows
and dries up, with a rhythm reckoned variously
in all the texts throughout the ages.

But He is also unchangeable,
and therefore seldom noticed here.
He crosses the path of march obliquely.

Like the vessel that passes through fog
without the fog observing a thing. Silence.
The lantern's slender shine is the signal.

Stones

Stones that we have thrown I hear
falling, glass-clear through the years. In the valley
fly the moment's chaotic
acts shrieking from
treetop to treetop. Made mute
in thinner air than that of the present, they glide
like swallows over mountain
and mountain, until they
reach the farthest plains
at the edges of existence. There fall
all our achievements
glass-clear
to no bottom
except within ourselves.